The Search for
Christian Unity

A popular version of the
Directory for the Application of Principles and Norms on Ecumenism

Catholic Bishops' Conference of England and Wales

© 2002 Catholic Bishops' Conference of England and Wales

www.catholic-ew.org.uk

Published in January 2002 by the Catholic Communications Service, 39 Eccleston Square, London SW1V 1BX. ccs@cbcew.org.uk

Printed by Hastings Printing Company Ltd, St Leonards-on-Sea

ISBN 0 905241 21 5

Contents

Foreword

I wish to wholeheartedly commend this popular version of the *Ecumenical Directory*. The ecumenical journey is, as I have said, a 'road with no exit'.

It is my sincere hope that through the study of this document the work of ecumenism will be given new impetus in dioceses and parishes. As the Pope recently said, the journey may sometimes seem a long one but 'The invocation *"ut unum sint"* is ... a binding imperative, the strength that sustains us. ... It is on Jesus' prayer ... that we base the hope that even within history we shall be able to reach full and visible communion with all Christians' (*Novo Millennio Ineunte*, n. 48).

Cardinal Cormac Murphy-O'Connor
Archbishop of Westminster
President, Bishops' Conference of England and Wales

Introduction

This is a shortened version of the *Directory for the Application of Principles and Norms on Ecumenism* which was issued by the Pontifical Council for Promoting Christian Unity in 1993. The 1993 *Directory* is much fuller than the earlier versions published in 1967 and 1970. Not only does it give Vatican II's teaching on ecumenism (especially in the Decree *Unitatis Redintegratio*), but it also gathers together the teaching, legislation and guidance issued since that time by successive Popes, the Holy See and the *Code of Canon Law*. Our shorter version focuses mainly on those parts of the 1993 *Directory* judged by the editors to be of more immediate concern to clergy and laity at 'grassroots' level, and tries to present the material in a way which is both accurate and readily accessible. In preparing the text we also consulted with our ecumenical partners via the Theology and Unity Group of Churches Together in England.

This shortened version is published under the authority of the Catholic Bishops' Conference of England and Wales. Nevertheless, it must be stressed that only the full *Directory* is the official and authoritative text. This was approved by Pope John Paul II on 25 March 1993, and signed by Cardinal Cassidy, then the President of the Pontifical Council for Promoting Christian Unity, and by Bishop Duprey, the Secretary. The English translation was published by the Catholic Truth Society in 1993.

The text that follows is based entirely on the *Directory* itself, but in a few places a short editorial explanation is inserted. These are printed in square brackets, thus: [ie. traditions other than the Eastern Orthodox].

The *Directory* frequently uses the expression 'Churches and Ecclesial Communities'. 'Ecclesial Communities' are communities which the Catholic Church sees as having some, though not all, of the necessary elements of the Church of Christ. Either by their own desire or the practice of Vatican II they are not called 'Churches'. In this shorter directory we simply say 'Churches and Communities', or more briefly still, 'traditions'.

How to use this directory

This shortened version of the *Directory* gives a simplified text. The numbers at the end of each paragraph refer to the sections in the original document.

After each major topic there is a question or series of questions. These can be used for private reflection or, better still, for discussion in a small group. These questions are marked with a question mark.

At key points there are also suggestions 'for action', marked with an arrow.

At the end of each chapter is a list of 'keywords and ideas'. These give an overview of the main themes that have been discussed. They are followed by some suggestions for action or questions. This section is marked with an exclamation mark.

Preface

The Catholic Church has gathered a great deal of ecumenical experience over the last thirty years. This experience, together with the need for Catholics to play a greater part in ecumenism, means that accurate teaching and up-to-date discipline are called for. The *Directory* aims to provide this. (1-3)

The *Directory* is addressed first and foremost to the bishops who, with the Pope, are responsible for ecumenical policy, but it also concerns Catholics in general, who are called to pray and work for the unity of Christians. (4)

It should also be helpful to our brothers and sisters in other Christian Churches and Communities, so that they can better understand our ecumenical attitudes. (5)

The *Directory* has five chapters:
'*I. The search for Christian unity*' makes the Catholic Church's ecumenical commitment very clear.
'*II. Organisation in the Catholic Church at the service of Christian unity*' describes how the Church officially structures its search for unity.
'*III. Ecumenical formation in the Catholic Church*' deals with the vital issue of learning about ecumenism and forming an ecumenical attitude.
'*IV. Communion in life and spiritual activity among the baptised*' spells out appropriate ways of sharing in prayer and in both sacramental and non-sacramental worship.
'*V. Ecumenical co-operation, dialogue and common witness*' looks at practical details of working, witnessing and sharing in dialogue together.

I. The search for Christian unity

This chapter looks at why we must work for Christian unity

faith, hope
and love

Ecumenism is a response to the grace of God. It calls all Christians to *faith* in the kind of Church God wants, to *hope* that Jesus' prayer - 'May they all be one' - may one day be answered in its fullness, and to *charity* which is the Spirit's gift uniting all believers.

'The Second Vatican Council clearly asked Catholics to reach out in love to all other Christians with a charity that desires and works actively to overcome in truth whatever divides them from one another.' (9)

This chapter gives the teaching of the Catholic Church on ecumenism as developed at the Second Vatican Council in the 1960s and also afterwards. It forms the doctrinal basis of the whole *Directory*. (10)

The basis

The Church and its unity in the plan of God

all together

God is drawing all human beings, and all creation, into union with himself. To accomplish this the crucified and risen Christ is calling human beings into the new People of God, the Church. This Church embraces an immense variety of men and women. To establish this People, Christ called the twelve Apostles, with Peter as head, and gave them the task of preaching the Gospel, celebrating the sacraments, and leading the People of God in love. The Church continues to be served by the ordained ministry of bishops, priests and deacons. What holds the Church together are the bonds of faith and sacrament, and a ministry which is hierarchical. (11/12)

United in this way, the People of God forms a *communion* - to give it its Greek name, *koinonia*, 'fellowship'. From Vatican II, this idea of communion has had a powerful influence on official teaching about the Church. (11/12)

The Church as communion

in communion with God and with each other

Fundamentally this communion is fellowship with God - with the Father through Christ in the Holy Spirit. The fellowship reaches its fullness in heaven, but it is present here on earth as well. When Christians are united in faith, hope and love, in common teaching and sacraments, and in the guidance of their pastors, they are part of that communion. Each local diocese, gathered round its bishop, makes present, 'in this place', the one communion and Church of Christ. (13)

communion ... between dioceses

This communion is between dioceses as well as within them. This world-wide communion is maintained especially by the communion between the bishops, and between them and the Bishop of Rome, Peter's successor. (14)

communion ... for mission

Each local diocese has the mission from Christ to bring the good news of the Kingdom to more and more people, offering them this communion with God and with everyone who already shares in it. As each diocese carries out this mission, the prayer of Jesus is being fulfilled: 'Father, may they be one in us, as you are in me and I in you, so that the world may believe it was you who sent me' (*John* 17:21). (15)

At the same time this unity-in-communion also contains a rich diversity of peoples and cultures, across the world and across the centuries: Christ's Church is indeed 'catholic'. The very richness of this catholicity sometimes gives rise to tensions - but, in spite of these, the Spirit of God is always at work calling Christians, in all their diversity, to ever deeper unity. (16)

It is Catholic teaching that this one Church of Christ 'subsists' in the Catholic Church. What this means is that the whole of revealed truth, sacraments and ministry are found in it, although as individuals we Catholics do not make full use of these gifts of Christ. This Catholic teaching needs to be remembered when we refer to other Christian communities as 'other Churches and Communities', etc. (17)

~~~~~~~~~~~~~~~~~~~~~~~~~~~~~~~~~~~~~~

1. 'The Catholic Church embraces with hope the commitment to ecumenism as a duty of the Christian conscience, enlightened by faith and guided by love' (Pope John Paul II, *Ut Unum Sint*, 8). What does it mean to take seriously our duty to be committed to ecumenism?

2. How do you try to carry out the mission of the Church in your parish? How could you do it better with other Christians? (see para 15)

3. Paragraph 16 suggests that unity involves diversity. How can we have unity without uniformity?

4. Why are you a Catholic and not a member of a different tradition? What is it about the Catholic Church that you think is distinctive and valuable?

Where we stand now

Divisions among Christians and the re-establishing of unity

partial communion - how others relate to us

From the very beginning of the Church, folly and sinfulness weakened its unity, and rifts soon appeared, but much more serious divisions arose later on. The eastern Churches and the Church of the west divided, and then, in the west, deeper divisions emerged concerning discipline, doctrine and the nature of the Church. All the same, the communion between us, though damaged, has never been completely destroyed. While the fullness of unity belonging to the one Church of Christ has always remained in the Catholic Church, other Churches and Communities have still been in partial communion with us, and, as the Decree on Ecumenism, *Unitatis Redintegratio* (*UR*), puts it, 'The Spirit of Christ has not refrained from using them as means of salvation' (*UR*3). (18)

the ecumenical movement

At the same time, Christians should never be satisfied with these lesser forms of communion. They do not correspond to the will of Christ, and they weaken the Church in the exercise of its mission. In the twentieth century especially, the grace of God has moved members of many traditions to strive to overcome these divisions by prayer, repentance and meeting together. This is what is meant by 'The Ecumenical Movement'. (19)

defining unity

At Vatican II, the Catholic Church pledged itself to work for Christian unity. It defined this unity as 'confession of one faith ... the common celebration of divine worship ... the fraternal harmony of the family of God' (*UR*2). This kind of unity of its very nature requires the full visible communion of all Christians - in Catholic teaching this is

13

the ultimate goal of the ecumenical movement. This does *not* however mean that we have to sacrifice the great diversity that has grown up among Christians, as long as this diversity is faithful to the apostolic tradition. (20)

What do you think of the definition of unity in paragraph 20?

What can we do?

Ecumenism in the life of Christians

working for
unity

All who have been baptised in Christ's name are by that very fact called to commit themselves to the search for unity; to live our baptism is to take part in Christ's mission of making all things one. (22) Catholics, therefore, are invited to co-operate in this:

'Where ecumenical work is not being done, or not being done effectively, Catholics will seek to promote it. When it is being opposed or hampered by sectarian attitudes and activities that lead to even greater divisions ... they should be patient and persevering.' (23)

dangers and
possibilities

There are two opposite dangers here:
• indifferentism (ignoring important differences);
• proselytism (coercive persuasion).

When Catholics are in ecumenical contact with other Christians they need to:

14

- act honestly, prudently and with knowledge of the issues;
- know their own Church - its discipline and its ecumenical principles;
- have accurate knowledge of the Christian traditions they are dealing with. (23/24)

change of heart   Ecumenism gets right to the heart of Christian spirituality. It calls for 'a change of heart and holiness of life, along with public and private prayer for the unity of Christians' (*UR*8). After all, those who identify with Christ must identify with his prayer, above all his prayer for unity; those who lead a life of repentance will be sensitive to the evil of divisions and will pray for conversion; those who seek holiness will be able to recognise it also outside the visible boundaries of the Catholic Church. (25)

The different levels of ecumenical activity

Every level of the Church - parochial, diocesan, national and universal - has its appropriate forms and discipline for ecumenical work.

At *parish level*, for instance, the pain that is felt by families whose members belong to different traditions and cannot receive Holy Communion together can be an incentive to prayer and ecumenical effort.

At the *national level*, members of a Bishops' Conference should work together to develop effective ecumenical relations with other Christian traditions in their region. After all, they share the same culture.

At the *global level* it is for the whole College of Bishops with the Pope to make the necessary decisions about restoring full communion with other Churches, and for guiding ecumenical activity throughout the world. (26/29)

1. What have you learnt from the above section?

2. How can we avoid ecumenism becoming a search for the lowest common denominator?

3. What is the difference between encouraging people to join the Church (eg. through RCIA), and proselytism?

Complexity and diversity of the ecumenical situation

the bishop
Ecumenical situations can be diverse in the extreme, and at times quite unprecedented, so there is a special need for the apostolic ministry of the bishop, in order to encourage the disheartened and moderate the imprudent, and ensure that our ecumenical life is conducted on Catholic principles.

the whole church
When Catholics are in the majority it is obvious that the ecumenical scene will differ from when they are in the minority compared with other Christians. It will be different again when the majority population belongs to a non-Christian faith. Nevertheless, even when Catholics are in the majority, it is essential to be ecumenically active: the ecumenical movement needs to involve the whole Church. (30/32)

Sects and new religious movements

This describes a world-wide phenomenon today, which is very complex and varies enormously. In many cases these religious groups have little or no interest in fostering good relations with the Catholic Church. The local bishop must decide on the appropriate policy regarding the ones in his diocese. The principles of co-operation outlined in this *Directory* only apply to Churches and Communities which do have ecumenical relations with us. (35/36)

~~~~~~~~~~~~~~~~~~~~~~~~~~~~~~~~~~~~

Communion/*koinonia*
Unity not uniformity
Subsists
Change of heart/conversion
Ecumenism at all levels

Survey your parish and local ecumenical relationships

Take each of the words in turn
and ask yourself about ecumenism in your area

As a result, what do you notice?

~~~~~~~~~~~~~~~~~~~~~~~~~~~~~~~~~~~~

II. Organisation in the Catholic Church at the service of Christian unity

This chapter looks at who does what

our circumstances can help

In different parts of the world, Catholic dioceses often exist side by side with other Christian Churches and Communities, sharing with them a common spirituality, a common ethnic and cultural background, and a common political history. In addition, these other traditions often have their highest authority in regions corresponding to the territory of a particular Bishops' Conference. These circumstances can lead to very fruitful ecumenical relations and can benefit the ecumenical movement generally. (37-38)

who regulates?

Vatican II entrusted leadership in the Catholic ecumenical task to the bishops throughout the world: to the whole College of Bishops with the Pope for the world-wide Church, and to bishops or Bishops' Conferences for local dioceses and regions. It is, then, their responsibility to regulate the work of the persons or commissions that are described here. (39-40)

The diocesan ecumenical officer

the work of the officer

The bishop needs to appoint a competent person to fulfil this task. His/her responsibilities will include:

• animating the work of the diocesan ecumenical commission;

- encouraging diocesan initiatives concerning prayer for unity;
- seeing that ecumenical attitudes influence diocesan activity;
- representing the Catholic community in relation to other Christians and their leaders;
- facilitating contacts between other Christian leaders and the bishop, clergy and laity;
- advising the bishop and other members of the diocese on ecumenical matters;
- keeping in touch with ecumenical officers and commissions in other dioceses.

Even when personnel are scarce, or when Catholics are in the majority, it is still right to appoint an ecumenical officer for whatever ecumenical work may be appropriate. (41)

~~~~~~

Who is your diocesan ecumenical officer?

What does he/she do?

~~~~~~

You may want to write to the ecumenical officer perhaps to invite him/her to meet you, or to discover what resources for ecumenism may be available for use at local level.

~~~~~~

The diocesan ecumenical commission

the commission's membership and work

The bishop should set up a commission or secretariat to implement his ecumenical policy and promote ecumenical activity in the diocese. If necessary, several dioceses may jointly form such a commission. (42)

The membership should reflect the Church as a whole and include clergy, male and female religious, and laity with the relevant (especially ecumenical) skills. It would be a good idea to have representation from the diocesan council of priests, the pastoral council and the diocesan or regional seminary.

In general, the commission should co-operate with other groups or persons in the diocese that have an ecumenical purpose. It should be in contact with parishes, with religious communities and with lay organisations. It should be a support for the ecumenical officer. (43)

terms of reference

More specifically, the commission's terms of reference should include:

- putting into effect the decisions of the Church authorities on ecumenical matters;
- keeping in touch with the ecumenical commission of the whole Bishops' Conference;
- encouraging spiritual ecumenism;
- taking forward the ecumenical formation of clergy and laity by means of day conferences, seminars and the like;
- taking an interest in the way seminary students are being prepared for the ecumenical dimension of their future ministry;

- promoting good relations between Catholics and other Christians;
- initiating dialogue with other Christians at diocesan level;
- promoting joint witness to the Christian faith and co-operating with other Christians in such matters as education, peace and justice, and culture. (44)

Parishes, too, should be encouraged to take part in ecumenical initiatives at their local level, sharing their ecumenical experience with other parishes and with the diocesan authorities. (45)

~~~~~~~~~~~~~~~~~~~~~~~~~~~~~~~~~

Who are the members of the Diocesan Ecumenical Commission?

How could they help you?

~~~~~~~~~~~~~~~~~~~~~~~~~~~~~~~~~

Discover what the Commission does and the resources they may have to help your parish 'take part in ecumenical initiatives at local level'. (45)

~~~~~~~~~~~~~~~~~~~~~~~~~~~~~~~~~

The ecumenical commission of the Bishops' Conference

the task of the Bishops' Conference Committee for Christian Unity

Each Bishops' Conference needs to set up a commission of bishops for ecumenical affairs, assisted by experts (clerical, religious and lay), if possible with a permanent secretariat. This commission is to give guidance on ecumenical matters connected with the region. If the Conference is too small for a commission of bishops, at least one bishop should be given responsibility for overseeing the commission's work, which is as follows: (46)

- doing most of the things the diocesan commission (above) has to do, but for the wider territory;
- putting into effect any instructions from the Holy See;
- facilitating co-operation between diocesan ecumenical officers, and between commissions, across the region, and arranging meetings;
- assisting other commissions and sections of the Bishops' Conference to have an ecumenical dimension to their work;
- helping to set up dialogues and consultations with other Christian traditions at national level, and appointing qualified people to take part in them;
- keeping in touch with the ecumenical work of other groups, such as the religious orders and others in consecrated life;
- maintaining contact with the Bishops' Conference and with the ecumenical commissions of other Bishops' Conferences, and also with the Pontifical Council for Promoting Christian Unity. (47)

Religious orders and societies of apostolic life

the ecumenical work religious orders and societies should undertake

The particular commitments of these communities in the Church, and the circumstances in which they frequently live out these commitments, mean that they enjoy special opportunities for ecumenical thought and work. In a way that is consistent with their calling they should, for instance:

- raise awareness of the *ecumenical* importance of the religious life - conversion of heart, holiness, prayer, and service are at the very heart of the ecumenical movement;
- help people to realise the ecumenical aspect of the vocation of all Christians to a life of holiness, by offering guidance in spiritual formation, prayer and the service of others;
- arrange meetings among Christians for liturgical prayer, for retreats and spiritual exercises and for the deeper understanding of Christian spiritual traditions;
- develop relationships with religious communities in other Christian traditions, sharing experience and resources;
- collaborate with other Christians in working for social justice, peace and the care of creation, and in the fields of health and education.

These religious communities will naturally need to work within the ecumenical policy of the bishop and the Bishops' Conference, keeping contact as appropriate with their ecumenical commissions and with the Holy See.

It would be a good idea if the central authorities of these religious communities each appointed a delegate, or a commission, to foster their ecumenical commitment and to be responsible for ecumenical formation, advice and practical initiatives. (51)

~~~~~~~~~~~~~~~~~~~~~~~~~~~~~~~~~~~~~~~

1. If you are a member of a religious order how many of the above practical points are you involved in?

2. What more could your order do to forward the ecumenical journey?

3. If you are not a member of a religious order find out what religious congregations working locally are doing to forward ecumenism.

~~~~~~~~~~~~~~~~~~~~~~~~~~~~~~~~~~~~~~~

Organisations of the Catholic faithful

local organisations have a part to play

At every level in the Church, from the parochial to the international, there are organisations for spiritual renewal, peace and justice, education and economic aid. All these need to pay serious attention to the ecumenical aspects of their work. (52)

~~~~~~~~~~~~~~~~~~~~~~~~~~~~~~~~~~~~~~~

How far do our parish organisations 'pay serious attention' to the ecumenical aspects of their work?

~~~~~~~~~~~~~~~~~~~~~~~~~~~~~~~~~~~~~~~

If you are a member of a Catholic organisation (eg. SVP, UCM, CWL), find out who are your equivalents in other denominations locally. See if there are ways you could do some aspects of your work together.

The Pontifical Council for Promoting Christian Unity

the work of the Pontifical Council At the level of the universal Church, the Pontifical Council operates as a department of the Vatican, and its brief is that of promoting full communion among all Christians. It tries to promote an ecumenical spirit and ecumenical activity within the Catholic Church, and cultivates relations with other Churches and Communities. It is responsible for the proper interpretation of the Catholic principles of ecumenism; it arranges official dialogues at the international level; it appoints Catholic observers to various international ecumenical bodies. At times, it issues directives applicable to the entire Catholic Church. It maintains contact with bishops and with Bishops' Conferences and their ecumenical commissions. It is important that communication between these and the Pontifical Council should be a two-way affair, because this strengthens ecumenical life across the Church and intensifies communion within it. (53/54)

Catholic structures for ecumenism
Raising awareness
Developing relationships
Co-operation

What do these words mean in practice
in your local situation?

What *one* thing might you *do* as a result
of reading/studying this chapter?

III. Ecumenical formation in the Catholic Church

This chapter looks at learning about ecumenism and how we can develop an ecumenical attitude. There are four sections:
A. Formation of all the faithful
B. Formation of pastoral ministers (ordained and lay)
C. Specialised formation
D. On-going formation

everyone's concern

The search for Christian unity is everybody's concern in the Church: laity and clergy alike. All need to be educated and formed to play their appropriate part, and the means of such formation are already to hand in the Catholic Church. (55)

flexible approach

People and circumstances vary enormously, so methods of formation have to be 'tailored' and flexible. Ecumenism calls for a conversion of heart and a change of attitude, so those in charge need to proceed very sensitively and often very gradually. (56)

basic principles

When a scheme is being worked out for steadily developing ecumenical formation, whether for teachers or for those in pastoral ministry, there are some basic principles to bear in mind. There should be:

- from the very start, a deepening of biblical and doctrinal knowledge, together with a study of the country's history and its ecumenical situation;
- a study of the history of Christian divisions, and of the effort to heal them;

27

- a study of the doctrines of other Churches and Communities in their historical context;
- a study of theological dialogues and studies in common, with any clarification that has resulted.

This developing formation will lead those involved to distinguish real differences of principle from matters of legitimate diversity, and will prevent merely subjective interpretations of other Christians' belief and life, and indeed of Catholic doctrine itself. As the formation progresses, concern for the unity of the Catholic Church and concern for communion with other Christians should become two sides of the same coin, and quite inseparable. (57)

~~~~~~~~~~~~~~~~~~~~~~~~~~~~~~~~~~~~~

In the light of your own local situation put this list in order of priority *for action*. Decide how you will go about getting it started.

~~~~~~~~~~~~~~~~~~~~~~~~~~~~~~~~~~~~~

A. Formation of all the faithful

unity with Christ - the Church - other Christians

The gift of unity that Our Lord prayed for on the night before his Passion is something of fundamental importance for every member of the Church, imbued as each is with the Spirit of Christ.

- In the first place this unity is *our union with Christ himself* - in one movement of love that, through Christ, extends to the Father and to our neighbour;
- secondly, this unity is *our communion with the whole*

Church world-wide - through being in communion with the particular diocese we belong to;
• thirdly, this unity is *the fullness of unity we seek with all other Christians*. (58)

~~~~~~~~~~~~~~~~~~~~~~~~~~~~~~~~~~~

What is the connection between your own personal growth in holiness and Christian unity?

~~~~~~~~~~~~~~~~~~~~~~~~~~~~~~~~~~~

The means of formation

Hearing and studying the Word of God in the Bible

we are formed in different ways

Along with us, our fellow-Christians have a deep love and reverence for the holy scriptures; so if we study the Bible lovingly and listen to it with attention, one and the same Word of God will strengthen the path to unity. (59)

Preaching
The different parts of the liturgical year offer many opportunities for preaching on themes connected with unity. 'Preaching should concern itself with revealing the mystery of the unity of the Church, and, as far as possible, promoting visibly the unity of Christians.' (60)

Teaching the faith (catechesis)
Religious education (for the young and for adults) is a crucial time for forming ecumenical attitudes. To ensure that this happens, however:

• We must teach the whole of Catholic doctrine, firmly and charitably, and remember that some doctrines are nearer the very heart of Christian revelation than others (what is known as the 'hierarchy of truths').

• We must present the teaching and practices of other Christian traditions correctly and honestly, recognising that many very valuable elements of Christ's Church are found there, and that God uses these Churches and Communities as means of salvation. This will help us to see more clearly the truths we hold in common, deepen our own Catholic faith and better appreciate the faith of other Christians.

• Our religious education should arouse a real desire for unity, and a resolve to purify ourselves humbly of unnecessary obstacles that we might be putting in the way.

• We must make clear that a truth of faith can often be expressed in more than one way - because this can help ecumenical understanding and dialogue. (61)

Liturgy
The liturgy can make a positive contribution to the unity of Christians, because the liturgy both celebrates unity and furthers it. This is true above all of the Eucharist, so it is vital that the Mass be celebrated well, to give the faithful the best opportunity to be drawn into closer unity with God and with each other. Liturgical prayer for unity, such as the Votive Mass for Unity in the Missal, is an important resource as well; so are the unity services during the Week of Prayer in January or near Pentecost. These can all help to form ecumenical attitudes. (62)

The spiritual life
'Change of heart and holiness of life, along with public and private prayer for the unity of Christians, should be

regarded as the soul of the whole ecumenical movement' (*UR*8). To live a genuine spiritual life is already to share deeply in the ecumenical movement.

Catholics must learn to value the spiritual riches in other Christian traditions. These include the scriptures, some or all of the sacraments, the gifts of the Holy Spirit and the key virtues of faith, hope and charity. There is the mystical tradition of the Eastern Churches, their monastic life (and that of the Anglicans); there are the riches of Anglican worship and piety, evangelical traditions of prayer and the forms of Protestant spirituality. Catholics need to know all these much better and, where appropriate, be enriched by taking part in them. (63)

Other means of formation
Working together for the 'social Gospel', struggling together for human rights and in the cause of peace, sharing concern for the integrity of creation, are all formative of an ecumenical attitude, especially when there is joint reflection on the specifically Christian reasons for doing this. (64)

~~~~~~~~~~~~~~~~~~~~~~~~~~~~~~~~~~~~~

From this list of means of ecumenical formation which one do you think should come first?

Make a list in order of priority of what you could do in practice.

~~~~~~~~~~~~~~~~~~~~~~~~~~~~~~~~~~~~~

Where can formation flourish?

These are some of the places where human and Christian maturity, and the sense of companionship and communion, can grow. They are also the seed-bed of a welcoming ecumenical attitude: (65)

In the family
Vatican II called the family 'the domestic church'. In the family, day by day, unity is strengthened or weakened according to the quality of its loving and communion together. The ideal family is a community open to the Church and to society, and a community where prejudice is resisted.

Mixed marriages have a special responsibility here, as they endeavour to live out their common baptism across the divisions, and to be builders and examples of Christian unity through the quality of their life together. (66)

In the parish
The parish 'should be, and proclaim itself to be, the place of authentic ecumenical witness'. Through the preaching and catechesis that goes on in the parish the parishioners should be formed in the ecumenical spirit. Someone in the parish needs to be given responsibility for promoting and planning ecumenical activity, and collaborating with the parishes and congregations of other Christians. A parish, of course, should also witness to the unity of the Church by the quality of its own internal relationships, and the charity and mutual respect between its members. (67)

In the school
Schools of all types should have an ecumenical dimension to their RE syllabus. They should be training young hearts and minds in openness to dialogue and in the things that make for peace and good relationships. At the relevant level, the school should teach young people genuine ecumenism according to the doctrine of the Catholic Church, and other subjects, such as history or art, should be awake to ecumenical implications. Teachers, therefore, need to be adequately informed about the history and teaching of other Christian traditions. (68)

In Catholic associations
These ought not to be inward-looking, but open to consultation and the sharing of experience with similar bodies in other traditions, and, where it would help, eager to work with them. (69)

~~~~~~~~~~~~~~~~~~~~~~~~~~~~~~~~~~~~~

1. What have you discovered from this section?

2. What ideas do you see here for local initiatives?

~~~~~~~~~~~~~~~~~~~~~~~~~~~~~~~~~~~~~

Ecumenism is everybody's concern
Authentic ecumenical disposition
All need to be educated and formed
Growth through spirituality
Importance of the Bible
Importance of doctrine
Awareness of different methods of formation
Awareness of different places
Know your faith - know the faith of other Christians

In the light of the above and your consideration about
what action you will take as a result of this chapter,
what one thing will you do and when?

B. Formation of those in pastoral ministry

ORDAINED MINISTERS

candidates need to develop an ecumenical disposition

'The candidate for the ministry needs to develop fully those human qualities which make a person acceptable and credible among people, checking regularly his own language and capacity for dialogue, so as to acquire an authentically ecumenical disposition.' These qualities apply to permanent deacons as well as to bishops and priests. (70)

a) Doctrinal formation

part of the Catholic tradition

The ecumenical dimension in formation
Ecumenical activity has to be fully consonant with the faith the Catholic Church has always professed, yet open

to dialogue and free from subjective interpretations of either Catholic doctrine or that of other traditions. Students can therefore be confident that the unchanging dogmatic statements of the Church will always convey the revealed truth if we interpret them properly; yet they also need to learn the difference between the revealed truth itself and the historically conditioned ways of formulating it. They should appreciate the difference between the fundamental apostolic tradition and merely ecclesiastical traditions. They should also recognise that there can be a perfectly legitimate variation in theological language, so that formulations can often be complementary, not contradictory. The 'hierarchy of truths' (see 61) must always be respected - ie. not all the truths we hold by faith are equally central to the mystery revealed in Christ. (73-75)

The ecumenical dimension in theological formation

common Christian heritage

It is not merely a question of adding a course on ecumenism to the syllabus - each different subject should emphasise, where appropriate:

- our common Christian heritage of truth and holiness;
- the riches of spirituality, liturgy and doctrine proper to other traditions;
- points of disagreement, which encourage deeper exploration of the Word of God: this can help distinguish real contradictions from only apparent ones. (76)

The ecumenical dimension of individual theological subjects

ecumenism is part of the whole syllabus

Every subject on the theological syllabus should reveal a link with the mystery of the unity of the Church. A comparative approach like that in paragraph 76 should lead to an awareness of the riches of *whole* Christian tradition, and inspire fidelity to it. 'When students compare their own patrimony with the riches of the other Christian traditions of east and west, whether in their ancient or modern expression, they will become more deeply conscious of this fullness.' (77)

This is true of all the disciplines, right across the syllabus, from scripture and the Fathers through to pastoral and sociological studies: all of them can contribute to a greater sense of the fullness of the Christian tradition. (77-78)

A specific course on ecumenism

specific courses
on ecumenism
During seminary training there should be a compulsory course on ecumenism. A general introduction should come near the beginning of the curriculum, so that students will be more alive to the ecumenical dimensions of all that they study, and a full treatment towards the end so that it can be integrated into their whole theological formation.

The content will vary with circumstances, but topics such as these would be important:

- the notion of 'catholicity' (the Church as world-wide and all-embracing), and the Catholic understanding of the visible and organic unity of the Church;
- the doctrinal basis and justification for ecumenical activity - especially the real but incomplete communion that already exists between Christians;
- the history of our divisions and of the efforts to heal them - where we are at present;
- different forms and 'models' of unity;
- what the various Christian Churches and Communities

are like today, their life and structure, their spirituality, their doctrinal emphases, their forms of worship;

- spiritual ecumenism and prayer for unity;
- particular problems, such as shared worship, mixed marriages, the role of the laity (especially women) in the Church. (79-80)

It would, of course, be wise to invite lecturers and experts from other communities, especially to deal with the teaching and life of their own tradition. (81)

b) Ecumenical experience

experience as well as theory

Ecumenical formation of students ought not to be merely theoretical, but be related to the lived experience of other traditions. Meetings, socialising, discussion and dialogue could usefully be organised, including meetings between students for the ministry. Beyond this, authorities locally must make decisions because circumstances vary so widely. (82)

NON-ORDAINED MINISTERS AND HELPERS

a) Doctrinal formation

ecumenical education for all - for catechists and teachers

For lay catechists, teachers and other helpers, and in institutes of religious, pastoral and educational formation, the same type of programme and principles would apply as for ordained ministers - but adapted to the type of participant. (83)

- for religious communities

There are also the religious communities of various kinds. These too, in ways appropriate to them, need to share in the ecumenical life of the Church. Ecumenical formation should begin in the novitiate and continue throughout the time of formation. Every subject should have an ecumenical dimension, and there should be a specific course on ecumenism as well. Each religious institute should have a specialist trained in ecumenism, to be responsible for the ecumenical commitment of the whole institute. (84)

b) Ecumenical experience

- for lay people Laity with ecumenical responsibilities should be encouraged to develop contacts and exchanges with other Christian Churches and Communities. For religious, exchanges of information, or spiritual and even material help, could be organised with the monasteries and religious communities of other traditions. (85-86)

~~~~~~

If you are
• an ordained priest
• a deacon
• a seminarian or teach in a seminary
• a member of a religious order
• a catechist or in another lay ministry
what aspects of the above do you think you need to know more about?

~~~~~~

C. Specialised formation

The importance of formation for dialogue

Catholic universities, and other Catholic institutes of higher education, have a key role in preparing people who might later take part in official dialogue. Such dialogue will need:

- sincere faith commitment (otherwise dialogue becomes a mere academic exercise);
- a constant searching for new paths towards unity, through greater fidelity to the Gospel and the Christian faith;
- a conviction that official dialogue is not a private conversation, but is on behalf of the whole Church, so that it must be coherent with the Church's teaching;
- a respect for the convictions of one's dialogue-partners, and a recognition that they can help us to understand and explain their faith and life;
- a recognition that not everyone is equally qualified to take part in such dialogue, since there are varying degrees of education, maturity of mind and spiritual progress. (87)

Ecclesiastical faculties of theology

Ecumenical questions should be studied in the first degree course, and then again at the second degree level, where specialised courses in ecumenism should be offered. Naturally, the ecumenical dimension should be present throughout the whole programme. (88)

Catholic universities

There should be an ecumenical dimension whenever the subject calls for it. There can be ecumenical meetings and conferences, ecumenical matters treated in university journals, the fostering of good relations between Catholic and other Christian students, joint prayer and retreats in line with the principles of shared worship; and joint action in peace and justice issues. (89)

Specialised ecumenical institutes

There is a need, in every part of the Church, for institutes where research and teaching on ecumenism are conducted in co-operation with other Christians. These provide an important resource for the ecumenical work of the Church. (90)

[The meaning of this chapter on ecumenical formation is more fully developed in a document of the Pontifical Council for Promoting Christian Unity, *The ecumenical dimension in the formation of those engaged in pastoral work*, March 1998 - see *Briefing*, vol 28 no 3, 19 March 1998.]

D. On-going formation

up-dating

Both ordained and non-ordained ministers and workers for the Church need frequent up-dating in ecumenical affairs, because the scene is in constant development. Bishops and religious superiors should give careful attention to the systematic instruction of priests, religious, deacons and laity on the current state of the ecumenical movement. Ministers from other Churches can be invited to explain their own traditions, and to speak on pastoral issues which are so often common to all. Local and regional meetings of clergy have the potential to deepen relationships and enable problems to be worked on together. The seminaries and other theological institutions could offer opportunities for on-going formation. The media, especially the religious media, can provide a useful service by giving information on recent developments. Joint spiritual meetings and retreats, etc., give the opportunity to reflect and pray together about unity, share spiritual experience, and explore elements of spirituality which are held in common, as well as those specific to a particular tradition.

It is desirable that from time to time there be an evaluation of the ecumenical life of the diocese, religious community, etc. (91)

~~~~~~

Different but similar formation for varying types of ministry
Open to dialogue - develop contacts
Ecumenical dimension to study 'across the board'
Every subject should have an ecumenical dimension
Experience must go alongside theory

In the light of the above, what ecumenical formation, or in-service training, do you think you need most urgently?

~~~~~~

Pass on this request/information to the appropriate person in your diocese.

~~~~~~

IV. Communion in life and spiritual activity among the baptised

This chapter looks at appropriate ways of sharing in prayer and in sacramental and non-sacramental worship. It does this under three sections:
A. The sacrament of baptism
B. Sharing spiritual activities and resources
C. Mixed marriages

A. The sacrament of baptism

baptism is a beginning

By baptism a person is truly incorporated into Christ and into his Church, and is reborn to a sharing of the divine life: so baptism is the sacramental bond of unity among all who have received it. But baptism is only a beginning, for it is directed towards acquiring the fullness of life in Christ, and should lead to a complete profession of faith, a complete incorporation into Christ's system of salvation, and to Eucharistic communion. (92)

how baptism is conferred

Baptism must be conferred:
• with water
• with a formula clearly indicating that it is done in the name of the Father, Son and Holy Spirit.

It is essential that all Christian traditions celebrate baptism in this way, and that they agree as closely as possible about its significance and what is necessary for a valid baptism. There needs to be a dialogue between them, so as to reach a common understanding of the sacrament, a mutual recognition, and agreed procedures in cases of doubt. (93/94)

In reaching such common understanding, the Catholic tradition would want to say:

1. Baptism by immersion or by pouring, together with the Trinitarian formula, is of itself valid, so if a given tradition's liturgical books prescribe either of these methods the baptism must be considered valid - unless, in a particular instance, there are serious grounds for doubting that the minister has followed the ritual.

2. The minister's insufficient faith does not invalidate a baptism, as long as he/she intended to do what the Church does. This intention is presumed, unless there are serious grounds for doubting it.

3. Doubts sometimes arise on how the water was used, or whether it was used at all. The practice of merely sprinkling, especially over several candidates at once, can easily lead to doubts about validity. The normal practice of the tradition concerned should be investigated before a judgement is made. (95)

Catholics may join with other Christians in commemorating the baptism which unites them, and in renewing their baptismal promises. (96)

common baptism but into one particular church

Although baptism incorporates a person into Christ and his one Church, in practice this can only be into a given Church or Ecclesial Community. Accordingly, baptism cannot be conferred by two ministers of different traditions. It is perfectly in order, though with the bishop's permission:

• for the minister of another tradition to read a lesson, offer a prayer, etc., at a Catholic baptism;

- for a Catholic minister to do the same at a baptism in another tradition, if invited, provided that the celebration does not conflict with Catholic principles or discipline. (97)

~~~~~~

Even though we hold a common baptism, why does the Catholic Church say we cannot be a full member of two Churches?

~~~~~~

godparents - who and why

Godparents, in the strict canonical sense, should be members of the same tradition as that of the baptism. They are there not only for the candidate's Christian education, but to represent a faith community and to guarantee the candidate's faith and desire for membership. However, because of the closeness of faith between the Catholic Church and the Eastern Orthodox, a suitable Orthodox Christian may be a godparent, for a good reason, at a Catholic baptism as long as the other godparent is a Catholic and the candidate's Catholic education is provided for. Equally, a Catholic may be a godparent at an Orthodox baptism, if invited.

Because of our common baptism, and ties of blood and friendship, a member of another [ie. non-Eastern Orthodox] Christian tradition may be a witness [not technically a godparent] at a Catholic baptism, as long as there is a Catholic godparent as well. Equally, a Catholic may be a witness at a baptism in another tradition. (98)

All Christians have the right to be received into full communion with the Catholic Church, if in conscience they ask for it. In some circumstances it may then be necessary to ascertain the validity of their previous baptism. This is the procedure:

1. For Eastern Christians, their rite of baptism is certainly valid, so all that is needed is to establish the *fact* of the baptism. This would also cover confirmation, because (even if it is not mentioned on the certificate) in the Eastern tradition confirmation is administered with baptism.

2. For other Christians, if there has been an agreement on baptism with their Church or Community, all that is needed is to ascertain that baptism was celebrated according to that agreement. If an official certificate has been given there is no reason to doubt the validity, unless in a particular case there are serious reasons to do so. If there has been no agreement with the tradition in question, that should still not *automatically* lead to doubt.

3. If, after investigation, doubt persists, the Catholic minister will baptise conditionally, explaining what he is doing and why he is doing it. Such a baptism should be celebrated in private.

4. Bishops' Conferences should issue guidelines for the reception of baptised Christians, taking into account that they are not catechumens, and may already have considerable knowledge and experience of the Christian faith. (99-101)

distinguishing *baptised and* *non-baptised*	If baptised Christians are received at the Easter Vigil, there should be a clear distinction between them and those who are to be baptised. (100)
confirmation *before* *communion*	Regarding the sacrament of confirmation, there has been no agreement so far with the Reformation traditions, so Christians who are received from these traditions should be confirmed in the Catholic Church before they take their first Holy Communion. (101)

~~~~~~

1. How do you welcome people from other Christian traditions into your local situation?

2. What have you learnt from the above section?

~~~~~~

B. Sharing spiritual activities and resources

principles for *sharing*	Appropriate sharing is much to be encouraged, and includes such things as prayer, liturgical worship and the use of sacred things and places. There is a two-fold principle at work here:

1. We are *already in real communion* with all the baptised. The gifts which Catholic faith believes to be bestowed in fullness upon the Catholic faith (ie. the whole of revealed truth and all the means of salvation) exist in varying ways outside the Catholic Church's visible boundaries. Churches and

46

Communities not in full communion with us have significance and value in the mystery of salvation, because the Spirit of Christ uses them as means of salvation. So in varying ways their celebrations 'are able to nourish the life of grace ... and provide access to the communion of salvation' (*UR*3-4). This real communion between us can be expressed in shared prayer and liturgy.

2. We are *not yet in full communion*, because of differences of faith and understanding. Unrestricted spiritual sharing would be incompatible with this.

So rules are needed to allow for sharing which is appropriate to the different traditions.

(Note: Catholic priests are not permitted to concelebrate the Eucharist with ministers of *any* other tradition, because concelebration is a visible expression of full communion in faith, worship and community life.)

consult   There needs to be give and take ('reciprocity') about this sharing, because good will and charity are at the heart of it. There needs to be consultation between the authorities concerned to see how this can best work. (102-106)

'Catholics ought to show a sincere respect for the liturgical and sacramental discipline of other Churches and Ecclesial Communities and these in their turn are asked to show the same respect for Catholic discipline. One of the objectives of the consultation mentioned above should be a greater mutual understanding of each other's discipline and even an agreement on how to manage a situation in which the discipline of one Church calls into question or conflicts with the discipline of another.' (107)

~~~~~~

What do paragraphs 102-107 mean in practice in your area?

~~~~~~

Prayer in common

make the effort to pray with others

Catholics should be positively encouraged to pray with their fellow Christians. Such prayer in common is already a step towards unity. There are all kinds of needs we should pray for together: eg. for peace, for the family, for social concerns. It is right to pray together in times of crisis or thanksgiving, or when we are remembering those who have died for our country.

practical ideas

Prayer in common is most appropriate of all when we are praying for unity itself, such as during the Week of Prayer for Christian Unity. In planning unity services, representatives of all the traditions can get together, making use of their common heritage of hymns and prayers, but also of the riches belonging to the individual Churches. The venue can be either a church of one of the participants, or some other suitable place. The form of dress for those leading the service should be agreed beforehand. (108-113)

other ways

Other forms of spiritual sharing include days of recollection, retreats, and joint study of the various spiritual traditions. There may also be permanent associations for a deeper spiritual searching; but valuable though these are, our real differences of doctrine must not be forgotten, nor the Catholic Church's teaching about sacramental sharing. (114)

on Sundays? The celebration of the Eucharist on the Lord's Day is the foundation and centre of the whole liturgical year, that is why Catholics are obliged to attend Mass on that day. For that reason, it is better not to hold ecumenical services on Sundays, because Catholics would still have to go to Mass. (115)

~~~~~~

1. How do you celebrate the Week of Prayer for Christian Unity in your area?

2. What from these four sections could you do?

3. Does paragraph 115 cause difficulties locally? If so, how could these be tackled?

~~~~~~~~~~~~~~~~~~~~~~~~~~~~~~~~~~~~

Sharing in non-sacramental liturgical worship

unity services By 'liturgical worship' we mean worship according to the books and customs of a particular Church or Community, presided over by a minister or delegate of that tradition. The non-sacramental liturgy of a particular tradition will often be preferred to a specially constructed unity service. Catholics are encouraged to take part in these. In Catholic services of this kind (eg. Evening Prayer) other ministers may have the place and liturgical courtesies proper to their rank, and Catholic ministers may accept a similar invitation in the services of other traditions. (116-119)

funerals If their own minister is unavailable, Christians from another tradition may be given a Catholic funeral, unless it was clearly against their will. (120)

praying for
others

There can be prayers for other Christians, living or dead, during a Catholic liturgy, sacramental or non-sacramental (eg. the Intercessions at Mass); but it is an ancient tradition that during the Eucharistic Prayer only those in full communion with the Catholic Church are mentioned by name. (121)

~~~~~~~~~~~~~~~~~~~~~~~~~~~~~~~~~~~~~~~

Write a bidding prayer for next Sunday with ecumenism in mind. Whom would you include and why? (You might also like to include something in the parish newsletter or bulletin.)

It has been suggested that local congregations regularly pray for one another's particular needs during Sunday worship. Does this happen in your area? Could the practice be introduced?

~~~~~~~~~~~~~~~~~~~~~~~~~~~~~~~~~~~~~~~

Sharing in sacramental liturgical worship - especially the Eucharist

a) Sharing with members of the Eastern Churches.

respect the
discipline

There is a very close communion in matters of faith between the Catholic Church and the Eastern Churches. They possess true sacraments: above all, the priesthood and the Eucharist. This encourages liturgical sharing - even of the Eucharist - in the right circumstances. But the Eastern Churches may well have a stricter discipline, which we must respect. (122)

how to approach
an eastern church

A Catholic may ask the minister of an Eastern Church for the sacraments of penance, Eucharist and anointing of the sick, if there would be a genuine spiritual advantage and if a Catholic minister is only available with great difficulty. Indifferentism and the danger of error must be avoided. The Eastern discipline must be observed as far as possible regarding frequency, confession before Communion, and the Eucharistic fast. If the particular Eastern Church restricts Communion to its own members, a Catholic should not attempt to receive it. (123-4)

who can do what   Catholic ministers may give the sacraments of penance, Eucharist and anointing of the sick to Eastern Christians, if they freely ask for them and are properly disposed. There should be due consideration of the Eastern discipline, and no suggestion of proselytising. (125)

Catholics may read the lessons at Eastern sacramental liturgies and an Eastern Christian may do the same at Catholic sacraments. (126)

A Catholic minister may take part in an Eastern Church wedding, if invited, and a Catholic may be bridesmaid or best man. Equally, an Eastern Christian may be bridesmaid or best man at a Catholic wedding. (The general discipline of both Churches about taking part in such weddings must be observed, of course.) (127-8)

b) Sharing in sacramental life with Christians of other Churches and Communities

principles   There are two principles here that need to be kept in mind, and never separated:

1. A sacrament is an action of Christ and of his Body the Church. When a given community celebrates a sacrament it is both a sign and a source of that

community's unity in faith, worship and community life. So, for instance, *Eucharistic* Communion is inseparably linked to *'ecclesial'* communion (ie. the Church-fellowship.)

2. At the same time, baptism does bring members of other traditions into a real (though incomplete) 'ecclesial' communion with the Catholic Church, and baptism of its very nature is the beginning of a process. It is directed towards acquiring the fullness of life in Christ, and finally to full Eucharistic Communion, which is the food that unites us more and more deeply to Christ and his saving work.

In the light of these two principles, taken together, the Catholic Church *normally* restricts Holy Communion, penance and anointing of the sick to her own members. But *exceptionally* the same two principles enable the Church to permit (and even commend) access to these sacraments to other Christians in certain circumstances of grave and pressing need. (129)

practical
applications

What are these circumstances?

1. Danger of death - in danger of death, Catholic ministers may give these sacraments to baptised Christians of other traditions, provided that:

• their own minister is unavailable;
• they ask of their own accord;
• they manifest Catholic faith in the sacrament they desire;
• they are properly disposed.

2. Other circumstances of 'grave and pressing need' - each diocesan bishop is strongly recommended to

issue rules for judging other circumstances of grave need, and for verifying the conditions in paragraph 1 above. [The bishops of Britain and Ireland have done so, in their teaching document *One Bread One Body*, 1998, paras 95-117.] He should first take into account any rules the Bishops' Conference has issued, and consult with the other Churches and Communities of his own diocese. Catholic ministers will judge individual situations according to these rules, where they exist. Otherwise, they should judge according to the rules of this *Directory*. (130-1)

If Catholics are in grave need under the conditions listed above, they may only ask for these sacraments from a minister of a Church whose sacraments are valid in the eyes of the Catholic Church, or from someone who [ie. as an individual] is known to be validly ordained. (132)

The scripture lessons at a Catholic Eucharist should be read by a Catholic, but for a good reason the bishop may allow another Christian to do so. But a homily which is part of the liturgy itself is reserved to the priest or deacon, because it is the presentation of Christian faith and morals in accordance with Catholic teaching. (133-4)

At weddings, other Christians may be the chief bridesmaid or best man, and Catholics may do the same at weddings in other traditions. (136)

~~~~~~

Not being able to share fully in the Eucharist causes pain to all concerned. What can we do to help lessen it?

~~~~~~

Sharing other spiritual resources

buildings Catholic churches are normally reserved for Catholic worship, but if other Christians do not have a place of their own, or lack the liturgical objects, the bishop may allow the use of both. They may also, with permission, make use of Catholic cemeteries. (137)

shared ownership Where ecumenical relations are good, and financial and pastoral considerations seem to suggest it, serious thought could be given to the shared ownership of church premises, or shared use over a longer period. In these cases, consideration needs to be given to the reservation of the Blessed Sacrament, in view both of Catholic theology and the respect required, and of ecumenical sensitivity. There will need to be agreement about how the various disciplines are going to be observed, and a written agreement regarding financial matters and anything arising from civil or ecclesiastical law. (138-40)

schools In Catholic schools there must be respect for the faith and conscience of pupils and teachers from other traditions. Their clergy should be free to give spiritual and sacramental care to their own faithful. With the bishop's permission this can include the use of the school chapel. (141)

hospitals and homes Catholic hospitals and homes for the elderly should promptly inform the appropriate ministers of the presence of their members. They should offer every facility for dignified spiritual care, including the use of the chapel. (142)

~~~~~~~~~~~~~~~~~~~~~~~~~~~~~~~~~~~~~~

What possibilities do these paragraphs suggest for local ecumenical action in your area?

~~~~~~~~~~~~~~~~~~~~~~~~~~~~~~~~~~~~~~

C. Mixed marriages

'Mixed marriage' here means any marriage between a Catholic and a baptised Christian not in full communion with the Catholic Church. (143)

difficulties   The Church's first concern is to uphold the indissoluble bond of marriage and the family life that flows from it. This is easier to achieve when both partners belong to the same Christian faith community; mixed marriages often give rise to difficulties regarding Christian commitment and family harmony. In principle, then, marriage between people of the same tradition is the thing to be encouraged. (144)

values   At the same time, the number of mixed marriages has grown, and even though they have their difficulties they have very valuable aspects too, and they can make a real contribution to the ecumenical movement. This is particularly the case when both partners are faithful to their religious duties. (145)

support and encourage   The Church and especially her ministers and their assistants have a special responsibility for instructing and supporting Catholics in mixed marriages, to help them live their faith. They must also care for the couple as such, in marriage preparation, in the wedding itself, and in the married life afterwards. Bishops could usefully draw up guidelines for this pastoral care. (146)

If possible, this pastoral care should be carried out jointly with the minister of the other tradition. (147)

preparation During marriage preparation, there should be great emphasis on the positive riches the couple share as Christians, and they should be encouraged to foster all that can lead to unity. Yet they also need to be faithful to their own commitment, and not 'paper over' real differences. They would be advised to learn about their partner's personal religious convictions, as well as those of his/her Church or Community. They should recognise the fundamental importance of praying together as a means of spiritual harmony and the usefulness of reading the scriptures together. (148-9)

what about the The couple have to be instructed on the essential
children? purposes and nature of marriage, and they must not exclude these. The Catholic partner will be asked to affirm that he/she is prepared to avoid the dangers of abandoning the Catholic faith, and to do all in his/her power to have their children baptised and brought up in the Catholic Church. The partner from the other tradition must be told of the Catholic's responsibilities, but no formal promise is required of him/her. Indeed, this partner may feel a similar but opposite obligation.

They should be invited to discuss the Catholic baptism and upbringing of the children, and if possible come to a decision on the matter, before they marry. An explicit refusal by the non-Catholic partner will be one factor to be considered - among others - when the bishop or his delegate decides on a dispensation. (150)

The Catholic parent must do his/her duty of passing on the Catholic faith to the children, but with a proper respect for the other parent's conscience and regard for the stability of the family and the marriage. If, in spite of his/her best efforts, the children are not baptised and brought up as Catholics, the Catholic must still share the Catholic faith in other ways, by contributing to the Christian atmosphere of the home, by being well informed about Catholicism and ready to explain it, and by praying with the family for Christian unity. (151)

1. What questions, or areas, arising from this section need to be raised as people prepare for marriage?

2. How can we support people in mixed marriages?

Invite a local member of the Association for Inter-Church Families to meet with you or talk to the appropriate people in your parish.

between Catholics and Eastern Christians

Although doctrinal differences prevent full communion with the Eastern Churches, there is in both traditions a sound and consistent teaching of the faith, and the presence of true sacraments. So in the pastoral care of marriages between Catholics and Eastern Christians those in either Church can be assured that the children will, in any case, be nourished by the sacramental mysteries of Christ. Family prayer can be enriched by the diversity of liturgy and devotion that will be available to them. (152)

unlawful but valid

A Catholic is obliged to marry before a Catholic priest or deacon, plus two other witnesses. This obligation is called 'canonical form'. If a Catholic marries in an Eastern Orthodox Church without a dispensation from 'canonical form', he/she acts unlawfully, but the marriage is valid. But if a Catholic marries in any other tradition without dispensation, the marriage is invalid, as well as unlawful. (153)

the wedding

The bishop may dispense the Catholic from this for a serious reason, eg. to preserve family harmony. But the marriage must still be public in nature, and the exchange of consent must be expressed *once* only, at *one* religious service where *one* presiding person receives the marriage vows.

The bishop may permit a Catholic priest or deacon to attend such a wedding, and they may accept the presiding person's invitation to offer prayers, read from the scriptures, give a brief address, and bless the couple. Similarly, at a Catholic wedding, the bishop may permit the presiding priest or deacon to extend the same invitation to a minister of the other tradition. (154-8)

A mixed marriage normally takes place outside Mass, because of problems with Eucharistic sharing for witnesses and guests, though for a good reason the bishop may permit a Nuptial Mass. In this case, the decision on giving Holy Communion to the non-Catholic spouse must be governed by the rules explained earlier, bearing in mind that two baptised Christians celebrating the sacrament of marriage are in a very special situation. (159)

inter-
communion?

Even though the husband and wife in a mixed marriage share two sacraments - baptism and marriage - in their married life Eucharistic sharing can only be exceptional. The rules about sharing outlined earlier must be observed. (160)

~~~~~~

Common baptism
Membership
Real but partial communion
Prayer in common
Prayer for each other
Appropriate and specific circumstances
Support for mixed marriages

What have you discovered from this chapter?

Will you be taking any action?

~~~~~~

V. Ecumenical co-operation - dialogue - common witness

This chapter looks at the practical aspects of working, talking and sharing together.

do everything together which is allowable

When Christians live and pray together as in chapter IV, they are witnessing to the faith they share, to their baptism and to their fellowship of life and gifts. But there are many other forms of ecumenical co-operation that express and promote this fellowship, and enhance the witness to the Gospel's saving power before a world in need of Christ. The contribution Christians can make to all the areas of life where the need of salvation is manifested will be more effective when they make it together, and are seen to be doing so. *Hence they will want to do everything together that is allowed by their faith.*

We are limited in what we can do by divergence in teaching, by wounded memories and by a long history of separation - but co-operation can help overcome these barriers and it can reveal what already unites us. (161-2)

The form or structure that ecumenical co-operation can take varies a great deal, of course, from the short-term 'one-off' meeting to permanent councils and committees. We turn to the latter now. (163-5)

Councils of Churches and Christian Councils

getting together

Councils of Churches [and, in the four nations of Britain and Ireland, 'Churches Together'] consist precisely of those: Churches and 'Ecclesial Communities'. Christian Councils have a wider membership. The purpose of both is to facilitate dialogue, common work and witness, the overcoming of misunderstanding, and prayer. The only authority they have is that accorded to them by their constituent bodies. Since these Councils are an important form of co-operation it is a welcome development that the Catholic Church is increasing its contacts with them. (166-7)

The decision to join a Council, and the oversight of Catholic participation in it, is the responsibility of the bishop or bishops of the territory in question. While bishops are considering whether to join they should be in touch with the Pontifical Council for Promoting Christian Unity. (168)

not churches in themselves Before deciding to join a Council, bishops need to be sure that their membership of it will not blur the unique and specific identity of the Catholic Church, and that it is compatible with the Catholic Church's understanding of itself. Councils are not, and must not try to become, Churches in themselves. The voting system, the decision-making process, the manner of making public statements and the degree of authority attributed to such statements, together with the system of representation, all need to be clearly settled before Catholic membership is decided on. (169)

Catholic membership of these Councils is quite distinct from the relationship between the Catholic Church and the World Council of Churches. The latter does not have authority over these Councils. (170)

a serious responsibility Deciding to join is to take on a serious responsibility, and the Catholic Church needs to be represented by well-qualified and committed people. (171)

1. What is the name of your local 'Churches Together' (or Council of Churches) or equivalent?

2. What does it do?

3. Who are its members?

4. How involved is your church?

Ecumenical dialogue

openness is necessary

Dialogue necessitates openness about oneself, and trust in what others say about themselves. It is a listening and a questioning, and a readiness to be questioned. One must be ready to clarify one's views further, and to modify one's personal views and behaviour. It enables the participants to identify the areas where they are in accord and where they differ. They try to discover the roots of these differences, and then assess whether they are really obstacles to a common faith. When they *are* real obstacles, they try to overcome them in the light of the faith they already hold in common. (172)

types of dialogue

Local dialogue can range from the most informal and every-day conversation, to organised discussions among various classes of people (professional people, clergy, theologians, etc.). Then there are formal dialogues between representatives specifically appointed by the Churches. Before the results of the formal dialogues can engage the Church officially, the authority appointing the representatives must give its approval. Catholics who take part need to be well informed about their faith, and careful to represent the Church faithfully. (173-5)

As Vatican II says (*UR*11), the manner and order in which Catholic truth is expressed should not be obstacles to agreement, though of course the Catholic position must be presented clearly and fully. But it does need to be in words and ways that our dialogue-partners can understand. Catholics in dialogue must remember the 'hierarchy of truths': while all revealed truth demands the same acceptance of faith, some truths are nearer than others to the foundations of the Christian message. (176)

The report of a dialogue commission will have intrinsic weight because of the competence of its authors, but it will not be binding on the Catholic Church until the authorities of the Church have approved it. (177-8)

The members of the People of God must, at their various levels, be involved in the process of judging an Agreed Report, and thus exercise the *'sensus fidei'* (the God-given grasp of the faith). So every effort must be made to bring the results of dialogues to the attention of all Church members, together with the necessary explanations. It is to be hoped that every Church or Community involved in the dialogue will do the same - and indeed other traditions too. Not just the *doctrine* of faith, but the *life and prayer* of faith must enter into the process of *'reception'*, by which the whole Church makes its own the results of dialogue, in a process of listening, testing, judging and living. (179-180)

If an Agreed Statement is expressing the faith in a new (or newly discovered) way, this can enrich the Church. As Vatican II taught (*UR*6), the revealed truth itself is one thing, and the particular way it has been formulated is another. It is useful, though, that this new language should avoid ambiguity ['fudge'], especially when seeking agreement on points that were traditionally controversial. (181)

Faculties of theology have an important part to play in the process of reception - and the final judgement must be made by the Church's teaching authority. (182)

~~~~~~~~~~~~~~~~~~~~~~~~~~~~~~~~~~~~~

1. What makes for good dialogue?

2. What principles would you lay down for dialogue?

3. What do you know about the Agreed Statements already produced (eg. those with the Anglicans and with the Methodists)?

~~~~~~~~~~~~~~~~~~~~~~~~~~~~~~~~~~~~~

Common Bible work

the scriptures - a fundamental bond

Veneration of the scriptures is a fundamental bond of unity between Christians. If Christians read the Word of God, and do so together, it will strengthen this bond of unity and enable them to be more open to the unifying action of God. Everything should be done to encourage this joint Bible study. Work together in producing suitable editions of the Bible would be a great help here - and a witness in itself. (183)

study together and discover new things

Catholics should share in this study of the scriptures, all the way from local parish-groups to professional biblical scholars. This combined work can reveal how our different doctrinal positions, and our different approaches to the Bible itself, can lead to different interpretations of the Bible text. At the same time, Catholics will certainly learn from the experience and the traditions of the different Churches. They will see certain passages in a new light, and discover God's Word anew. They will experience with joy the unifying power of God's Word, and will be encouraged, together with their fellow Christians, to find its meaning in relation to the world of today. (184-6)

~~~~~~~~~~~~~~~~~~~~~~~~~~~~~~~~~~~~~
You have been asked to organise a Bible study on 'common witness'. What text would you choose and how would you organise the session?
~~~~~~~~~~~~~~~~~~~~~~~~~~~~~~~~~~~~~

Common liturgical texts

agree common liturgical resources

Christians in the same cultural area should agree a common version of at least the most important prayers, psalms and scripture readings. A common collection of hymns, and co-operation in producing liturgical music, would be desirable as well. (187)

Co-operation in catechesis

co-operation in catechesis where possible

Co-operation in catechesis can certainly enrich the Catholic Church's own life, and that of the other traditions. It is also a valuable form of common witness to the Gospel. All the same, collaboration in this field can only be limited: there are differences between us, and sometimes profound ones. In any case, catechesis is not just about teaching doctrine; it is about initiating someone into the whole Christian life, with a full sharing in the sacraments of the Church. (188)

65

Co-operation in institutes of higher studies

Co-operation in theology and related disciplines contributes to research, enriches theological education, and strengthens the ecumenical formation of clergy and other pastoral workers. It also enables Christians to address together the intellectual challenges of the day. (191)

In the first stages of theological education, students are still receiving their basic formation in the faith and tradition of their own Church. For Catholics, the teachers of these first-level doctrinal courses, including the introductory course on ecumenism (see paragraphs 79-80), should be Catholics themselves. Nevertheless, there can be ecumenical co-operation in other ways, even at this level. Catholic students could, for instance, attend courses at the theological colleges of other Churches and Communities, bearing in mind the usefulness to them of the course in question, the quality and ecumenical attitude of the teacher, and the maturity of the students. (192-4)

After the basic theological formation is complete, and at second and third degree level, visiting lecturers from other traditions could well be invited to give courses on the doctrinal positions of the Churches and Communities they represent. Catholic lecturers could well be invited to reciprocate. Much of this would depend on the maturity of ecumenical relations in the country concerned. (195)

At levels beyond this (ie. theological lecturers, etc.) a much wider field of ecumenical collaboration is possible. Here we are talking about theological specialists sharing their research, and a sharing of libraries, premises and other resources. There are in some countries Catholic institutes specifically geared to ecumenical theology and practice - all the better if they can co-operate with similar institutes of other traditions, and have members of other traditions on their staff. Elsewhere, there are institutes that are ecumenically run, for specific purposes such as relations with other faiths, or the scriptures, or indeed the whole field of ecumenism. (196-202)

Pastoral co-operation in special situations

collaboration in particular situations - hospitals, etc.

Ecumenical collaboration can be very effective in the pastoral care of hospitals, prisons, the armed forces, universities, industry and the world of the media. Catholics working in such ecumenical chaplaincies need to co-ordinate with the pastoral structures of their local Church, and respect the Catholic Church's ecumenical norms especially regarding sacraments and worship. (204)

Co-operation in missionary activity

co-operate in mission

All ecumenical collaboration is a missionary witness, of its nature, but we can give ecumenical witness in the work of evangelisation itself. We can co-operate in mission because of our common baptism and the heritage of faith that we share. Catholics would want all who are called to Christian faith to join with them in that fullness of communion they believe to exist in the Catholic Church, yet we must still rejoice at the work of God's grace when other Churches and Communities draw people to faith and baptism. (205-6)

do not 'spread' our divisions to new areas

As long as the evangelising work of other Churches and Communities is not sectarian or anti-Catholic, Catholics can join in supporting the missionary work of all the traditions together. In the case of missions outside

Europe there must be every effort not to transplant to new areas the human and cultural factors in our original European divisions. Where it is necessary to make clear the points of faith or morals where we differ, it must be done with mutual respect and love. We should nourish new converts in the ecumenical spirit, but avoid indifferentism or confusion. (207)

mission together
at home

It is certainly necessary to co-operate in the mission to the post-Christian people of our own secularised world. Our common witness to central Gospel truths can be a powerful invitation to a renewed interest in Christianity. We should be studying together the phenomena of atheism, materialism and secularisation, and the ways of relating the Gospel to our multi-cultural world. (208-9)

~~~~~~~~~~~~~~~~~~~~~~~~~~~~~~~~~~~~

1. If we are to engage in united witness what are the central Gospel truths we would want to proclaim?

2. Have you any experience of witnessing to the Christian faith together with members of other Christian traditions? If so, what was good about it? If not, what *could* be done in your area?

~~~~~~~~~~~~~~~~~~~~~~~~~~~~~~~~~~~~

Co-operation in the dialogue with other religions

dialogue with
non-Christians
together

Ecumenical contact with our fellow Christians, with the aim of Christian unity, differs radically from dialogue with the other religions. [The word 'ecumenism' refers to the search for unity *between Christians*: the search for closer understanding between Christianity and other world religions is called 'inter-religious' or 'inter-faith' dialogue.] Yet our contact with these other religions influences, and is influenced by, our ecumenical relations. Dialogue with other religions is something we Christians should be doing together. This is particularly true of Christian/Jewish relations, where we can all struggle with them against anti-Semitism and fanaticism. Christians as a whole can collaborate with other religions in promoting, for religious reasons, family life, respect for minorities, peace and justice. (210)

~~~~~~~~~~~~~~~~~~~~~~~~~~~~~~~~~~~~~

 In the light of this paragraph what should you be doing in your area?

~~~~~~~~~~~~~~~~~~~~~~~~~~~~~~~~~~~~~

Collaboration in social and cultural life

together for justice and peace Christians need to collaborate in promoting the dignity of the human person, the blessings of peace and a Christian spirit in science and the arts. They need to collaborate in the struggle against famine, illiteracy and poverty, and the unequal distribution of wealth. But all this collaboration has to go alongside the other forms of ecumenism mentioned earlier, especially *prayer*. Otherwise the efforts become a sectional interest and an ideology, and an obstacle to unity. (211-12) Here are a few specific examples of collaboration. They are not exhaustive: (213)

a) Common study of social and ethical questions
Groups could be set up to witness to basic Christian and human values - i.e. 'Christian humanism'. They could study, eg. the meaning of human work, the value of life,

religious liberty, and the forces that threaten such things, such as poverty, racism, consumerism, terrorism. The tradition of Catholic social teaching has a valuable contribution to make here. (214)

b) Co-operation in the issues of human need,
*   development and the stewardship of creation*
Development is a response to need, but development must show good stewardship. Catholics must play their part in the study and combating of things threatening the integrity of creation, such as uncontrolled industrialisation. The whole area of development should be ecumenically addressed at all levels, such as promoting the dignity of women, peace, and a more just society. In global emergencies the Catholic Church encourages the pooling of resources and co-operation with all the relevant agencies, Christian and otherwise. (215)

c) Co-operation in the field of medicine
In poorer parts of the world, ecumenical collaboration in providing health care is essential. There is also the field of medical ethics - both a challenge and an opportunity in ecumenical work. Identifying human and Christian values is particularly vital here, when research is developing so rapidly, eg. in genetics. The Catholic Church's doctrinal stand has to be made clear, and the difficulties this creates for ecumenical co-operation have to be honestly faced. (216)

d) Co-operation in the media
Co-operation is needed to infuse Christian principles into the media industry, and to educate Christians in the critical use of the media.

There can be joint advisory bodies, joint TV and radio programmes, joint educational projects and professional training. There could be common use of satellites and cable TV networks. The formation of Catholic communicators should include a significant ecumenical preparation. The opportunities for co-operation are enormous! (217-8)

~~~~~~

Co-operation
Dialogue between Christians
Receiving from other traditions
Common work/witness/study
Role of Churches Together
Inter-faith dialogue

What have you discovered from this chapter?

In the light of this chapter,
what other examples of collaboration
do you think are possible (expecially locally)?

~~~~~~

And finally ....

What will you do about ecumenism now?

Further reading

Below are some suggestions for further reading and study, compiled by the Committee for Christian Unity.

Church documents
Second Vatican Council documents of particular interest are the Dogmatic Constitution on the Church, *Lumen Gentium*, and the Decree on Ecumenism, *Unitatis Redintegratio*. These can be found, along with the rest of the Council documents, in A Flannery (ed.), *Vatican Council II* volume 1 (Dominican Publications 1996).

The Search for Christian Unity is based on the 1993 *Directory for the Application of the Principles and Norms of Ecumenism* which remains the definitive text for further study. It is published in the UK by the Catholic Truth Society (CTS).

Essential reading for anyone involved in ecumenism is Pope John Paul's 1995 encyclical *Ut Unum Sint*. It is available from the CTS.

The issue of sacramental sharing, especially in regard to the Eucharist, is the subject of the 1998 teaching document of the bishops of England, Wales, Ireland and Scotland, *One Bread One Body*. This is also available from CTS.

Dialogue statements
The process of dialogue - bilateral and multilateral - has resulted in a large number of agreed statements and reports of one sort or another - far too many to list here. However, there are a number of collections available:

H Meyer & L Vischer (eds.), *Growth in Agreement: Reports and Agreed Statements of Ecumenical Conversations on a World Level* (Paulist Press 1984) includes the ARCIC I documents and the Lima Report 'Baptism, Eucharist and Ministry'.

J Gross, *Growth in Agreement II: Reports and Agreed Statements of Ecumenical Conversations on a World Level 1982-1998* (Eerdmans 2000), picks up where the previous volume left off.

W G Rusch & J Gross, *Deepening Communion: International Ecumenical Documents with Roman Catholic Participation* (Paulist Press 1998), fills in some gaps in the other volumes.

Theological works

It is somewhat risky to identify a couple of useful books. However, when reflecting on issues of church and ecumenism many teachers find the following titles useful to their students:

A Dulles, *Models of Church, Expanded Edition* (Image Books, 1987)

F Sullivan, *The Church We Believe in: One Holy Catholic and Apostolic* (Paulist Press, 1988)

Internet

A great way to find out about another denomination is to access their web sites - all major denominations have them and the best way to find them is to use a search engine. For ecumenical resources, including links to many documents, the Centro Pro Unione site is invaluable. It can be found at www.prounione.urbe.it .

Index

RECENT PUBLICATIONS

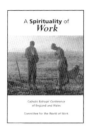

A Spirituality of Work

A Spirituality of Work, produced by the Committee for the World of Work of the Bishops' Conference of England and Wales, brings together prayers and Church teachings on work.

Chapter 1, 'Work in the sacred scriptures', examines the place of human work in God's plan since the beginning.

Chapter 2, 'The Church's teaching on work', outlines the development of the Church's teaching on work, particularly as expressed in the Second Vatican Council and in the writings of the modern popes.

Chapter 3, 'Human dignity and the value of work', explores this further, in the context of human dignity and the wider society.

The fourth chapter provides prayers and meditations for individuals and for use in groups and church services, and a final section is a list of further Catholic resources.

A Spirituality of Work, A5, 52 pages, £2.50,
ISBN 0 905241 18 5.

All publications available from
Catholic Bishops' Conference of England and Wales
39 Eccleston Square London SW1V 1BX

RECENT PUBLICATIONS

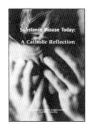

Substance Misuse Today: A Catholic Reflection

Substance Misuse Today: A Catholic Reflection, produced by the Social Welfare Committee of the Bishops' Conference of England and Wales, outlines how the Church might respond, both as a whole and locally, to the problem of drugs and alcohol misuse.

Substance Misuse Today covers the spiritual aspects of addiction, social context, drugs prevention, parish and family support, education and treatment, crime and prisons, sport and image. It also provides practical guidance for those approached by addicts, and an appendix of useful contacts.

Substance Misuse Today: A Catholic Reflection, A4, 52 pages, £3.00, ISBN 0 905241 16 9.

Briefing

Briefing is the official monthly journal of the Catholic Bishops' Conferences of Great Britain. It contains documents, information and news from the Church in Britain, Rome and overseas; official documents from the official sources.

£29.50 annual subscription.

Teachers of the Faith: speeches and lectures by Catholic bishops

Six cardinals and three other bishops have contributed to a unique collection of speeches and lectures, entitled *Teachers of the Faith*. All of the lectures were delivered in Britain over the last 26 years, and have appeared in the pages of *Briefing*, the official monthly journal of the Catholic bishops of Britain.

- **Cardinal Basil Hume** speaks about his personal faith journey and Jesus Christ today.
- **Cardinal Thomas Winning** discusses the Church in the third millennium.
- **Cardinal Cahal Daly**'s two contributions concern Northern Ireland, and the moral challenges facing the Church.
- **Cardinal Joseph Ratzinger**'s address is on consumer materialism and Christian hope.
- **Cardinal Johannes Willebrands** asks, is Christianity anti-Semitic?
- **Archbishop Derek Worlock** reflects on Catholic education and the 1944 Education Act.
- **Bishop Alan Clark** discusses the movement to Christian unity.
- **Bishop James Sangu** of Tanzania examines justice in the African context.

Teachers of the Faith: speeches and lectures by Catholic bishops, A5, 160 pages, £6.00, ISBN 0 905241 19 3